# Air Fryer Cookbook

# For TWO

## 60 Simple & Tasty Budget Friendly

# Recipes for Two with NO Oil

**William Garcia**

# Table of Contents

# Introduction

Preparing your favorite home meals is an integral part of everyday life. Barbecue wings, French fries, hamburgers – it's difficult to imagine modern life without these dishes. However, most of these dishes are harmful to our health because of the high content of fats and cholesterol. Constantly eating these dishes can cause heart problems, excessive weight and other difficulties. This is all due to the large amount of oil that is used when frying.

Solve this problem, reduce the amount of fat and at the same time get delicious food will allow a unique kitchen unit – the air fryer. This is a modern device, which is available in almost every kitchen, but many of us still do not know how to use it and what benefits it can bring to our life.

An air fryer is a kitchen appliance that cooks by circulating hot air around the food. A mechanical fan circulates the hot air around the food at high speed, cooking the food and producing a crispy layer via the Maillard effect.

Traditional frying methods induce the Maillard effect by completely submerging foods in hot oil. The air fryer works alternatively by coating the desired food in a thin layer of oil while circulating air heated up to 400-450 °F to confer energy and initiate the reaction. By doing this the appliance is able to fry foods like potato chips, chicken, fish, steak, French fries or pastries while using between 70% and 80% less oil than a traditional deep-fryer. This is great for your health and can significantly lower the level of cholesterol in the blood and reduce belly fat. In other words, air fryer is a must-have appliance in contemporary kitchen. So clean the dust from your air fryer and let's start creating! In this cookbook you'll find numerous air fryer recipes for you and your family to prepare amazing and easy air fryer recipes for any budget!

# Cooking Measurement Conversion Chart

## Liquid Measures

1 gal = 4 qt = 8 pt = 16 cups = 128 fl oz
½ gal = 2 qt = 4 pt = 8 cups = 64 fl oz
¼ gal = 1 qt = 2 pt = 4 cups = 32 fl oz
½ qt = 1 pt = 2 cups = 16 fl oz
¼ qt = ½ pt = 1 cup = 8 fl oz

## Dry Measures

1 cup = 16 Tbsp = 48 tsp = 250ml
¾ cup = 12 Tbsp = 36 tsp = 175ml
⅔ cup = 10 ⅔ Tbsp = 32 tsp = 150ml
½ cup = 8 Tbsp = 24 tsp = 125ml
⅓ cup = 5 ⅓ Tbsp = 16 tsp = 75ml
¼ cup = 4 Tbsp = 12 tsp = 50ml
⅛ cup = 2 Tbsp = 6 tsp = 30ml
1 Tbsp = 3 tsp = 15ml

Dash or Pinch or Speck = less than ⅛ tsp

## Quickies

1 fl oz = 30 ml
1 oz = 28.35 g
1 lb = 16 oz (454 g)
1 kg = 2.2 lb
1 quart = 2 pints

| U.S. | Canadian |
|------|----------|
| ¼ tsp | 1.25 mL |
| ½ tsp | 2.5 mL |
| 1 tsp | 5 mL |
| 1 Tbl | 15 mL |
| ¼ cup | 50 mL |
| ⅓ cup | 75 mL |
| ½ cup | 125 mL |
| ⅔ cup | 150 mL |
| ¾ cup | 175 mL |
| 1 cup | 250 mL |
| 1 quart | 1 liter |

## Recipe Abbreviations

Cup = c or C
Fluid = fl
Gallon = gal
Ounce = oz
Package = pkg
Pint = pt
Pound = lb or #
Quart = qt
Square = sq
Tablespoon = T or Tbl
        or TBSP or TBS
Teaspoon = t or tsp

## Fahrenheit (°F) to Celcius (°C)

$°C = (°F - 32) \times 5/9$

| Fahrenheit | Celcius |
|------------|---------|
| 32 °F | 0 °C |
| 40 °F | 4 °C |
| 140 °F | 60 °C |
| 150 °F | 65 °C |
| 160 °F | 70 °C |
| 225 °F | 107 °C |
| 250 °F | 121 °C |
| 275 °F | 135 °C |
| 300 °F | 150 °C |
| 325 °F | 165 °C |
| 350 °F | 177 °C |
| 375 °F | 190 °C |
| 400 °F | 205 °C |
| 425 °F | 220 °C |
| 450 °F | 230 °C |
| 475 °F | 245 °C |
| 500 °F | 260 °C |

## OVEN TEMPERATURES

WARMING: 200 °F
VERY SLOW: 250 °F - 275 °F
SLOW: 300 °F - 325 °F
MODERATE: 350 °F - 375 °F
HOT: 400 °F - 425 °F
VERY HOT: 450 °F - 475 °F

*Some measurements were rounded

9

# Breakfast Recipes

## Potato Bites with Cheese

**Prep time**: 20 minutes

**Cook time**: 25 minutes

**Servings**: 2

**Ingredients**

- 2 large Russet potatoes, peeled and cut
- ½ cup parmesan cheese, grated
- ½ cup breadcrumbs
- 2 tablespoon all-purpose flour
- ¼ teaspoon nutmeg, ground
- 2 tablespoon fresh chives, finely chopped
- 1 egg yolk
- 2 tablespoon olive oil
- ¼ teaspoon black pepper, ground
- Salt to taste

**Directions**

1. In lightly salted water boil potato cubes for about 15 minutes.
2. Drain potatoes and mash them finely with the potato masher. Let them completely cool.
3. To the mashed potato add egg yolk, grated cheese, chives, and flour.
4. Season the mixture with ground pepper, nutmeg, and salt.
5. Make 1 ½ inch balls and place them in the flour and then to the breadcrumbs.
6. Preheat the Air Fryer to 370-390 F
7. Cook potato rolls for about 10 minutes, until they become golden brown.

# Air Fryer Spinach Frittata

**Prep time**: 5 minutes

**Cook time**: 10-12 minutes

**Servings**: 2

**Ingredients**

- 1 small onion, minced
- 1/3 pack (4oz) spinach
- 3 eggs, beaten
- 3 oz mozzarella cheese
- 1 tablespoon olive oil
- Salt and pepper to taste

**Directions**

1. Preheat the Air fryer to 370 F
2. In a baking pan heat the oil for about a minute.
3. Add minced onions into the pan and cook for 2-3 minutes.

4. Add spinach and cook for about 3-5 minutes to about half cooked. They may look a bit dry but it is ok, just keep frying with the oil.
5. In the large bowl whisk the beaten eggs, season with salt and pepper and sprinkle with cheese. Pour the mixture into a baking pan.
6. Place the pan in the air fryer and cook for 6-8 minutes or until cooked.

# Delicious English Breakfast

**Prep time**: 5 minutes

**Cook time**: 13-15 minutes

**Servings**: 4

**Ingredients**

- 8 chestnut mushrooms
- 8 tomatoes
- 4 eggs
- 1 clove garlic, halved
- 4 slices smoked bacon, crushed
- 4 chipolatas
- 7 oz baby leaf spinach
- 1 tablespoon extra virgin olive oil
- Salt and ground black pepper to taste

**Directions**

1. Preheat the Air fryer to 390 F

2. Place the mushrooms, tomatoes, and garlic in a round tin. Season with salt and ground pepper and spray with olive oil. Place the tin, bacon, and chipolatas in the cooking basket of your Air Fryer. Cook for 10 minutes.
3. Meanwhile, wilt the spinach in a microwave or by pouring boiling water through it in a sieve. Drain well.
4. Add the spinach to the tin and crack in the eggs. Reduce the temperature to 300 F and cook for couple minutes more, until the eggs are prepared.
5. Sprinkle with freshly chopped herbs you prefer and serve.

# Sandwich with Prosciutto, Tomato and Herbs

**Prep time**: 2-3 minutes

**Cook time**: 5 minutes

**Servings**: 2

**Ingredients**

- 2 slices bread
- 2 slices prosciutto
- 2 slices tomato
- 2 slices mozzarella cheese
- 2 basil leaves
- 1 teaspoon olive oil
- Salt and black pepper for seasoning

**Directions**

1. Take 2 pieces of bread. Add prosciutto on the top. Add mozzarella cheese.

2. Place the sandwich into the Air Fryer and cook for 5 minutes in 380°F without preheating.
3. Using a spatula remove the sandwich.
4. Drizzle olive oil on top. Season with salt and pepper, add tomato and basil.

# Easy Breakfast Casserole

- Prep time: 15 minutes

- Cook time: 25-30 minutes

- Servings: 5-6

**Ingredients**

- 1 pound hot breakfast sausage
- ½ bag (15 oz) frozen hash browns, shredded
- 1 cups cheddar cheese, shredded
- 4 eggs
- 1 cup milk
- ¼ teaspoon pepper
- ¼ teaspoon garlic powder
- ¼ teaspoon onion powder
- ½ teaspoon salt

**Directions**

1. In the large skillet cook sausages until no longer pink. Drain fat.

2. Add shredded hash browns to the skillet and cook until lightly brown.
3. Place hash browns in the bottom of oven proof pan, lightly greased. Top with sausages and cheese.
4. It the bowl whisk together eggs, salt, pepper, garlic powder, onion powder, and milk.
5. Pour egg mixture over the hash browns.
6. Preheat the Air Fryer to 350-370 F
7. Place the pan in the fryer into the fryer and cook for 25-30 minutes, until become ready.

# Delicious English Breakfast

**Prep time**: 5 minutes

**Cook time**: 13-15 minutes

**Servings**: 4

**Ingredients**

- 8 chestnut mushrooms
- 8 tomatoes
- 4 eggs
- 1 clove garlic, halved
- 4 slices smoked bacon, crushed
- 4 chipolatas
- 7 oz baby leaf spinach
- 1 tablespoon extra virgin olive oil
- Salt and ground black pepper to taste

**Directions**

6. Preheat the Air fryer to 390 F

20

7. Place the mushrooms, tomatoes, and garlic in a round tin. Season with salt and ground pepper and spray with olive oil. Place the tin, bacon, and chipolatas in the cooking basket of your Air Fryer. Cook for 10 minutes.
8. Meanwhile, wilt the spinach in a microwave or by pouring boiling water through it in a sieve. Drain well.
9. Add the spinach to the tin and crack in the eggs. Reduce the temperature to 300 F and cook for couple minutes more, until the eggs are prepared.
10. Sprinkle with freshly chopped herbs you prefer and serve.

# Breakfast Sandwich

**Prep time**: 5 minutes

**Cook time**: 7 minutes

**Servings**: 1

**Ingredients**

- 1 egg, beaten
- 2 streaky bacon stripes
- 1 English muffin
- A pinch of salt and pepper

**Directions**

1. Beat 1 egg into an oven proof cup or bowl.
2. Preheat the Air fryer to 390°F
3. Place the egg in the cup, bacon stripes and muffin to the fryer and cook for 6-7 minutes.
4. Get the sandwich together and enjoy.

-

# Mac & Cheese with Topping

**Prep time**: 20 minutes

**Cook time**: 5 minutes

**Servings**: 3-4

**Ingredients**

- 3 cups macaroni
- 15 pcs Ritz biscuits
- 2 oz gruyere cheese, grated
- 2 oz butter
- 2 tablespoon plain flour
- 16 oz milk
- 1 clove garlic, minced
- 1 cup pizza cheese mix (Mozzarella, Parmesan, Cheddar)

**Directions**

1. Crush Ritz biscuits, mix with gruyere cheese and set aside.

23

2. Cook macaroni until almost ready, drained and also set aside.
3. Melt the butter in the separate bowl on the small fire and fry the garlic until fragrant. Add plain flour. Add milk and stir until mixture thickens and looks like a creamy soup. Add remained gruyere cheese and let it melt in the sauce.
4. Bring this sauce to a simmer and switch off the fire. Add macaroni into the mixture and combine well.
5. Dish into individual ceramic bowls.
6. Spoon with Ritz biscuits mixture over macaroni. Top with pizza cheese mix.
7. Preheat the air fryer to 350 F
8. Place ceramic bowls into the Air Fryer and cook for 5 minutes or until pizza cheese mix becomes golden.

# Side & Entrees

## Spicy Potato Wedges

**Prep time**: 10 minutes

**Cook time**: 20 minutes

**Servings**: 2-3

**Ingredients**

- 1 pound potatoes
- 1 tablespoon olive oil
- 1 tablespoon Provencal herbs
- Salt to taste

**Directions**

1. Cut potatoes into equal-sized wedges.
2. Soak potatoes for at least 30 minutes in cold water.

3. Place potato wedges into another bowl and evenly sprinkle with Provencal herbs, olive oil, and salt.
4. Preheat the air fryer to 370 F
5. Cook potato wedges for 15 minutes or until become ready and golden.
6. Serve with sour cream.

# Asparagus Spears Rolled with Bacon

**Prep time**: 10 minutes

**Cook time**: 9 minutes

**Servings**: 3-4

**Ingredients**

- 1 bundle asparagus, 20-25 spears
- 4 slices bacon
- 1 garlic clove, crushed
- 1 tablespoon olive oil
- 1 ½ tablespoon brown sugar
- ½ tablespoon toasted sesame seeds

**Directions**

1. Combine olive oil, brown sugar, and crushed garlic.
2. Separate bundle of asparagus into four equal-sized bunches and wrap each in a bacon slice.
3. Cover asparagus bunches with oil mixture.
4. Preheat the Air Fryer to 340-360 F

5. Put bunches into the air fryer and sprinkle with sesame seeds.
6. Cook for approximately 8 minutes.

# Mini-pigs in Blankets

**Prep time**: 10 minutes

**Cook time**: 10 minutes

**Servings**: 3-4

**Ingredients**

- 1 tin (8 oz) mini frankfurters
- 4 oz puff pastry
- 1 tablespoon smooth mustard plus some more for serving

**Directions**

1. Dry frankfurters with paper towels.
2. Cut the puff pastry into 2x1-inch strips.
3. Spread the stripes with mustard.
4. Preheat the Air Fryer to 370 F
5. Wrap each sausage with pastry stripes.
6. Put them into the fryer and cook for nearly 10 minutes or until they will become golden.

29

# Fried Tofu Cubes

**Prep time**: 10 minutes

**Cook time**: 20 minutes

**Servings**: 3-4

## Ingredients

- 12 oz low-fat Tofu
- 2 tablespoon soy sauce
- 2 tablespoon fish sauce
- 1 teaspoon sesame or olive oil
- 1 teaspoon Maggie

## Directions

1. Cut tofu into 1 inch cubes, place in the medium bowl and set aside.
2. Combine all ingredients and make a marinade.
3. Dip tofu to the marinade for at least 20-30 minutes.
4. Preheat the Air Fryer to 370 F

5. Cook tofu cubes for 15 minutes. If you want extra crispy cubes, cook for 5-10 minutes more.

# Spicy Grilled Tomatoes

**Prep time**: 5 minutes

**Cook time**: 20 minutes

**Servings**: 2

**Ingredients**

- 2 large tomatoes, sliced
- Herb mix (parsley, oregano, basil, thyme, rosemary or something else)
- Ground pepper and salt to taste
- 1 tablespoon olive oil or cooking spray

**Directions**

1. Cut tomatoes in half. Turn halves cut side up. Sprinkle tops with olive oil or cooking spray. Season with ground pepper and herbs dried or fresh.
2. Cook tomato halves in the air fryer for 20 minutes at 330 F.

# Broccoli with Cheddar cheese

**Prep time**: 10 minutes

**Cook time**: 12 minutes

**Servings**: 3-4

### Ingredients

- 1 head broccoli, steamed and chopped
- 1 tablespoon olive oil
- 1 – ½ cup Cheddar cheese, grated
- 1 teaspoon salt

### Directions

1. Steam the broccoli, cool after that and separate pieces from the stem.
2. Combine broccoli florets with grated cheddar cheese.
3. Preheat the Air Fryer to 340-360 F.
4. Place broccoli and cheese mixture to the blender, pulse couple times.
5. Form balls from the mixture with your hands, about 1 inch in diameter.

33

6. Place broccoli balls into the air fryer, sprinkle with oil and cook for 10-12 minutes.
7. Remove the balls, sprinkle with salt and serve with sour cream, or any sauce you like.

# Mashed Potato Tots

**Prep time**: 15 minutes

**Cook time**: 12-15 minutes

**Servings**: 2

## Ingredients

- 1 large potato
- 1 teaspoon onion, minced
- 1 teaspoon oil
- Salt and black pepper to taste

## Directions

1. Boil peeled potato over high heat.
2. Once the potato is almost ready remove it from the water. (It needs to be slightly harder than you need for mash)
3. Mash potato and mix with minced onion and oil. Season to taste.
4. Preheat the Air Fryer to 370 F

5. Make tater tots from the potato mixture and cook them in the air fryer for about 7 minutes. Shake once and cook for another 3-5 minutes.

# Brussels Sprouts with Pine Nuts & Raisins in Orange Juice

**Prep time**: 30 minutes

**Cook time**: 20 minutes

**Servings**: 4

**Ingredients**

- 1 pound Brussels sprouts
- 2 tablespoon raisins
- Juice and zest of 1 orange
- 2 tablespoon pine nuts, toasted
- 1 tablespoon olive oil

**Directions**

1. Put sprouts to the boiling water and cook for 4-5 minutes, then plunge in cold water, drain and set aside.
2. Squeeze juice from the orange and soak raisins in it for 15-20 minutes.

3. Preheat the Air fryer to 370 F. Combine sprouts in oil and roast for about 15 minutes.
4. Serve with raisins, pine nuts, and orange zest.

# Turnip Fries

**Prep time**: 5 minutes

**Cook time**: 30 minutes

**Servings**: 2

**Ingredients**

- Small turnip
- 1 tablespoon garlic powder
- 1 tablespoon Cajun spice
- 1 tablespoon olive oil

**Directions**

1. Cut turnip into nearly ¼ inch x 3-inch stripes.
2. Sprinkle with olive oil and spices, mix well.
3. Preheat the air fryer to 350 F.
4. Cook turnip strips for 25-30 minutes until golden and crispy.

# Spicy Green Beans with Pears and Peanuts

**Prep time**: 8 minutes

**Cook time**: 20 minutes

**Servings** 3-4

**Ingredients**

- 1 pound green beans
- 2 middle pears, not too ripe
- Fresh sage
- 2 tablespoons peanuts
- 3 fl oz low-fat whipping cream
- 3 fl oz vegetable stock
- 1 tablespoon vegetable oil

**Direction**

1. Trim the ends of beans and cut them into 2-inch strips.
2. Preheat the air fryer to 330 F. Pour beans and sage with olive oil and cook for 10 minutes.

3. Add diced pear and peanuts; pour in vegetable stock and low-fat whipping cream.
4. Cook for another 10 minutes.

# Crispy Zucchini Drumsticks

**Prep time**: 10-12 minutes

**Cook time**: 22 minutes

**Servings**: 4

## Ingredients

- 3 medium-sized zucchini, cut into thick one size sticks
- ½ cup breadcrumbs
- 2 egg whites
- 2 tablespoon Parmesan cheese, grated
- Ground black pepper
- Salt (or garlic salt)

## Directions

1. Combine breadcrumbs and grated parmesan cheese in a medium bowl.
2. Season zucchini drumsticks with salt and pepper, dip them into egg whites and evenly coat with breadcrumbs mixture.

3. Preheat your Air Fryer device to 380 F.
4. Put covered zucchini sticks into the fryer and cook for 15 minutes.

# Baked Cheesy Crescents

**Prep time**: 15 minutes

**Cook time**: 15 minutes

**Servings**: 4-5

## Ingredients

- 1 pound ground beef
- 8 oz cream cheese softened
- 2 cans crescent rolls
- Salt and pepper to taste

## Directions

1. In the skillet prepare ground beef until becomes ready. Drain fat.
2. In the bowl mix cooked ground beef and cream cheese. Season the mixture with salt and pepper to taste.
3. Separate rolls into triangles. Cut each triangle in half length-wise.
4. Scoop a heaping tablespoon into each roll and roll up.

5. Preheat the Air Fryer into 370 F
6. Bake for 15 minutes until crescents become golden and ready.

# Fried Cheese

**Prep time**: 5 minutes

**Cook time**: 15 minutes

**Servings**: 2

**Ingredients**

- 4 slices of white bread or brioche if you have one
- ¼ cup butter, melted
- ½ cup sharp cheddar cheese

**Directions**

1. Cheese and butter put in two bowls. On the each side of the bread brush the butter, and on two of sides put cheese.
2. Grilled cheese put together with bread and all put into the Air fryer at 360 F for 5-7 minutes.

# Asparagus Fries with Parmesan

**Prep time**: 10 minutes

**Cook time**: 10 minutes

**Servings**: 3

**Ingredients**

- 15-20 asparagus spears
- ½ cup flour
- 1 egg, beaten
- ½ cup whole grain breadcrumbs
- ½ cup parmesan cheese, grated

**Directions**

1. Dip the asparagus spears in the flour and shake off the excess.
2. Then dip them into the beaten egg and then into the breadcrumbs.
3. Preheat the Air Fryer to 390 F

4. Place coated asparagus spears into the air fryer basket and cook for 10 minutes.
5. Remove them and sprinkle with grated parmesan cheese on the top.
6. Cook for another 3-5 minutes until cheese becomes golden brown.

# Potatoes with Garlic and Coriander

**Prep time**: 5 minutes

**Cook time**: 30 minutes

**Servings**: 3-4

**Ingredients**

- 1 - 1/2 pound potatoes, peeled
- 2 tablespoons fresh coriander leaves, chopped
- 2 garlic cloves, chopped
- 2 tablespoon of olive oil
- Salt to taste

**Directions**

1. Peel potatoes and cut into cubes.
2. Mix olive oil, chopped garlic and coriander leaves.
3. Preheat the air fryer to 340 F.
4. Cook potato cubes for 35 minutes, until golden, then pour oil mixture over the potatoes and cook additionally for 5 minutes. Salt to taste and serve.

# Stuffed Mushroom Caps

**Prep time**: 10 minutes

**Cook time**: 5 minutes

**Servings**: 3

**Ingredients**

- 10 mushrooms
- 4 bacon slices, cut
- ¼ middle onion, diced
- ½ cup cheese, grated
- Ground black pepper and salt to taste

**Directions**

1. Wash mushrooms, drain well and remove stems.
2. Combine bacon, cut into ½ inch pieces, diced onion and grated cheese.
3. Season mushroom caps with salt and pepper.
4. Put bacon mixture to the seasoned mushroom caps.
5. Preheat the Air Fryer to 380 F

50

6. Place mushrooms into the air fryer and cook for 5 minutes until cheese melted.
7. Serve and enjoy.

# Cheesy Hasselback Potatoes

**Prep time**: 10 minutes

**Cook time**: 45 minutes

**Servings**: 3-4

**Ingredients**

- 10 medium sized potatoes
- 4 oz cheese, sliced
- 3 tablespoons olive oil
- 1 tablespoon fresh chives, chopped
- Salt and ground pepper to taste

**Directions**

1. Cut washed potatoes thinly without cutting completely/
2. Sprinkle with olive oil and season with ground pepper and salt to taste.
3. Preheat the Air Fryer to 360 F

4. Place potatoes to the fryer and bake for 30-35 minutes.
5. Insert cheese slices into each potato and sprinkle with chopped fresh chives.
6. Cook for another 3-5 minute until cheese becomes golden.
7. Serve with sour cream.

# Bubble & Squeak

**Prep time**: 3 minutes

**Cook time**: 23 minutes

**Servings**: 3-4

**Ingredients**

- Different leftover veggies (potato, sprouts, cabbage, etc)
- 1 medium onion, sliced
- 2 large eggs, beaten
- 3-4 slices turkey or chicken breast
- 2 oz cheddar cheese, grated
- 1 tablespoon mixed herbs or Italian seasoning
- 1teaspoon dried tarragon
- Salt and pepper to taste

**Directions**

1. Brake up your leftovers in the bowl. Add sliced onion and cheese, beat the eggs and season with herbs and salt.
2. Chop up the turkey and add it to the bowl and mix everything well with your hands or wooden spoon.
3. Preheat the Air Fryer to 370-380 F. Place the mixture into a baking dish and then place in the Air Fryer. Cook for 20-23 minutes until it is bubbling on top.
4. Sprinkle additionally with grated cheese and serve hot.

# Cheesy Baked Rice

**Prep time**: 5 minutes

**Cook time**: 25 minutes

**Servings**: 4

**Ingredients**

- 2 pack overnight cooked rice
- 1 tablespoon butter
- 4 garlic cloves, minced
- 3 tablespoon broccoli florets
- 1 medium-sized carrot, cubed
- 1 veal sausage, sliced
- 8-10 tablespoon creamy sauce
- 3 tablespoon shredded cheddar cheese
- 2 tablespoon shredded mozzarella cheese
- A pinch of salt to taste

**Directions**

1. Preheat the Air Fryer to 370 F.

56

2. Melt butter inside baking pan for about 1-2minutes. Sauté minced garlic for about 1-2 minutes or until fragrant. Then add in broccoli florets and carrot cubes and fry for 3-4 minutes. Add a little water will help to speed up the softening.
3. Add sausage slices and cook for 2-3 minutes or until they turn slightly browned. Add in the rice and mix well. Pour in the enough creamy sauce and mix well, level the rice with a ladle.
4. Sprinkle cheese evenly and air fry for 8 - 10 minutes.

# Poultry Recipes

## KFC Style Crispy Chicken Wings

**Prep time**: 30 minutes

**Cook time**: 30 minutes

**Servings**: 3

**Ingredients**

- 6-8 chicken wings
- Low-fat Greek yoghurt for marinade
- 1/2 teaspoon cayenne pepper
- 1/2 teaspoon white pepper
- 1 teaspoon garlic powder
- 1 teaspoon smoked paprika
- Salt to taste
- 1 teaspoon turmeric
- 1 oz flour
- 1 oz corn flour

## Directions

1. Combine all spices with Greek yoghurt and marinade chicken wings at least for 30 minutes.
2. Add extra spices you like to a mix of flour and maize flour in a large bowl.
3. Dip marinated wings into a flour mix and shake off.
4. Preheat air fryer to 350°F and sprinkle lightly with oil.
5. Cook for 30-35 minutes until golden.

# Balsamic Chicken with Vegetables

**Prep time**: 8 minutes

**Cook time**: 20 minutes

**Servings**: 4

**Ingredients**

- 8 chicken thighs
- 5 oz mushrooms, sliced
- 1 small onion, diced
- 8 asparagus spears
- 1 small carrot, diced
- 2 garlic cloves, minced
- ¼ cup balsamic vinegar
- 1 teaspoon sugar
- 1 teaspoon fresh rosemary
- 1 teaspoon dried oregano
- 1 teaspoon dried sage
- 1 tablespoon olive oil
- Salt and pepper to taste

**Directions**

1.  Sprinkle baking tray with olive oil.
2.  Rub chicken thighs with salt and pepper.
3.  Mix all vegetables in a large bowl. Add herbs, sugar, vinegar, mushrooms. Stir to combine.
4.  Replace vegetable mixture to the baking tray and also add chicken.
5.  Cook in the preheated air fryer for 20 minutes at 380 F.
6.  Serve.

# Chicken Marinated in Mustard

**Prep time**: 10 minutes

**Cook time**: 20 minutes

**Servings**: 2

**Ingredients**

- 4 chicken drumsticks
- 2 tablespoons brown sugar
- 1 teaspoon chili powder
- 2 garlic cloves, crushed
- 2 tablespoons  mustard
- 1 tablespoon olive oil
- Bundle of rosemary
- Ground pepper and salt to taste

**Directions**

1. Combine crushed garlic, chili powder, olive oil, brown sugar, and mustard. Season with salt and pepper to taste.

2. Dip chicken drumsticks to the marinade and leave for at least for 20-30 minutes.
3. Preheat the air fryer to 360-380 F
4. Cook for 10 minutes.
5. Then reduce temperature to 280-300°F and cook for another 10 minutes with lower temperature.
6. In 2-3 minutes before finishing add rosemary springs on the top of the drumsticks.
7. Serve warm with mashed potatoes or cooked rice.

# Chicken with Butternut Squash

**Prep time**: 10 minutes

**Cook time**: 20 minutes

**Servings**: 3

**Ingredients**

- 1/2 pound chicken breast
- 2 tablespoons sage leaves, chopped
- 1 teaspoon Worcestershire sauce
- 1/4 teaspoon salt
- 1 - 1/2 cups butternut squash, peeled and cut into 1/2 inch cubes
- 1 tablespoon vegetable oil
- 1 medium onion, sliced
- Freshly ground pepper

**Directions**

1. Cut chicken breast into 1-inch cubes and mix with Worcestershire sauce, salt and chopped sage leaves.

64

2. Peel butternut squash and cut into ½ inch cubes.
3. Preheat the air fryer to 350 F and cook squash drizzled with oil for 7 minutes.
4. Add onion and cook for another 3 minutes.
5. Mix in marinated chicken and cook for another 5-7 minutes until ready and golden.
6. Season with freshly ground pepper to taste.

# Bacon Wrapped Chicken

**Prep time**: 10 minutes

**Cook time**: 15 minutes

**Servings**: 2-3

### Ingredients

- 1 pound chicken tender, skinless and boneless
- 4-6 bacon stripes
- 4 tablespoon brown sugar
- ½ teaspoon chili powder

### Directions

1. Mix brown sugar and chili powder.
2. Cut chicken tenders into 2-inch pieces.
3. Wrap chicken pieces into bacon strips and toss with sugar mixture.
4. Cook wrapped chicken in the air fryer for about 10-15 minutes at 380 F.

# Whole Spicy Chicken with Rosemary

**Prep time**: 15 minutes

**Cook time**: 30 minutes

**Servings**: 3-4

**Ingredients**

- 1 whole chicken (4-5 pounds)
- 2 cups potatoes, diced
- ½ large onion, diced
- 3 garlic cloves, minced
- 1 ½ teaspoon black pepper
- 1 ½ teaspoon dried thyme
- 1 ½ teaspoon dried rosemary
- 1 ½ teaspoon dried paprika
- 2 teaspoon olive oil
- 1 ½ teaspoon salt
- Fresh rosemary and sliced lemon for decoration

**Directions**

67

1. Rub the whole chicken with 1 teaspoon salt and 1 teaspoon black pepper. Set aside for 20-30 minutes.
2. Mix diced potato and diced onion with ½ teaspoon salt and pepper, 1 teaspoon paprika, thyme, and rosemary.
3. In another small bowl mix olive oil, ½ teaspoon dried, ½ dried thyme, minced garlic.
4. Preheat the Air Fryer to 400 F
5. Stuff vegetable mixture into the chicken, and cover it with garlic sauce.
6. Wrap stuffed chicken with foil and cook in the air fryer for 30 minutes until chicken will become golden and ready.
7. Replace the chicken to the serving plate take potatoes and onion out of the chicken.
8. Decorate with lemon and fresh rosemary.

# Crispy Chicken Meatballs

**Prep time**: 20 minutes

**Cook time**: 14 minutes

**Servings**: 2-3

**Ingredients**

- 1 pound chicken breasts
- 1 large or 2 medium potatoes, pilled
- 1 medium carrot
- ½ green bell pepper, seeded and sliced
- 1 cup flour
- 2 tablespoons heated oil
- 1 teaspoon garlic paste
- ¼ teaspoon brown sugar
- 1 teaspoon chili powder
- Ground black pepper and salt to taste

**Directions**

1. Cut chicken breasts into ¼ inch pieces. Cover meat with garlic paste, season with salt and ground pepper and set aside for couple hours.
2. Mix flour, chili powder, brown sugar, heated oil. Stir to combine.
3. Cut potatoes, carrot and green bell pepper into ¼ inch pieces.
4. Add vegetables and marinated chicken into the flour mixture mix thoroughly, roll medium-sized meatballs and place them on a baking sheet.
5. Preheat the air fryer to 350-370 F
6. Place chicken meatballs in the fryer for 10-12 minutes until they become golden and crispy.
7. Serve with mayonnaise or your favorite dip sauce.

# Turkey with Pumpkin and Nutmeg

**Prep time**: 10 minutes

**Cook time**: 25 minutes

**Servings**: 4

**Ingredients**

- 1 pound boneless turkey breast, cut into cubes
- 1 pound pumpkin cut into cubes
- 4 tablespoons maple syrup
- 1 medium onion, sliced
- 1 bay leaf
- 1 sprig fresh thyme chopped
- 1 teaspoon nutmeg
- 6 tablespoons cherry jelly or cranberry sauce
- 2 cups chicken stock
- 2 tablespoons oil
- Salt and pepper

## Directions

1. Cut turkey into 1-inch cubes, slice onion, season and add to the air fryer. Cook for 5 minutes at 350 F until golden.
2. Add the maple syrup and set aside – let caramelize.
3. Cut pumpkin into 1-inch cubes. Add to the air fryer with nutmeg and cook together for 2-3 minutes.
4. Add chicken stock and herbs. Cook for 15 minutes.
5. Mix the sauce with cherry jelly and cook for another 2 minutes.

# Spicy Chicken Drumsticks with Garlic and Lemon

**Prep time**: 5 minutes

**Cook time**: 25 minutes

**Servings**: 3

**Ingredients**

- 1 pound chicken drumsticks
- 2 tablespoons chopped fresh coriander leaves
- 2 garlic cloves, chopped
- 3 tablespoons lemon juice
- 1 tablespoon vegetable oil
- Salt to taste

**Directions**

1. Put chicken drumsticks in the air fryer. Sprinkle with olive oil and cook for about 15-20 minutes at 350 F

2. Add coriander leaves and garlic, stir thoroughly. Sprinkle with freshly squeezed lemon juice and cook for another 5 minutes.

# BBQ Chicken

**Prep time**: 10 minutes

**Cook time**: 15 minutes

**Servings**: 3

- 1 pound chicken tenders
- ½ cup pineapple juice
- ½ cup soy sauce
- 4 garlic cloves, chopped
- ¼ cup olive oil
- 1 tablespoon fresh ginger, grated
- 4 chopped scallions
- A pinch black pepper
- 2 teaspoons toasted sesame seeds

## Directions

1. All ingredients mix in a large bowl and add chicken there. Set aside at least for 2 hours.
2. Preheat the air fryer to 390°F.
3. Cook for 5-7 minutes.

# Chicken Patties

**Prep time**: 20 minutes

**Cook time**: 15 minutes

**Servings**: 5-6

## Ingredients

- 1 pound chicken breasts
- 2 medium potatoes, peeled
- 1 small carrot, sliced
- 1 medium onion, sliced
- 1 cup all-purpose flour
- 3 tablespoon vinegar
- 1 teaspoon garlic powder
- ½ teaspoon chili powder
- Salt and black pepper to taste

## Directions

1. Cut chicken tenders into ¼ inch pieces. Season with salt, pepper and garlic powder, sprinkle with vinegar and set aside for 30 minutes.
2. Mix all ingredients in a large bowl. Add marinated chicken. Stir to combine.
3. Roll chicken patties with hands and cook in the air fryer for 8-15 minutes at 360 F, until brown and crispy.

# Meat Recipes

## Greek Meatballs with Feta

**Prep time**: 10 minutes

**Cook time**: 10 minutes

**Servings**: 3-4

**Ingredients**

- ½ pound ground beef
- 1 slice white bread, crumbled
- ¼ cup feta cheese, crumbled
- 1 tablespoon fresh oregano, chopped
- 1 tablespoon fresh parsley, chopped
- ½ teaspoon ground black pepper
- A pinch of salt

**Directions**

1. Combine ground beef, breadcrumbs, fresh herbs, ground pepper and salt. Mix well to receive smooth paste.
2. Divide the mixture into 8-10 equal pieces.
3. Wet your hands and roll meatballs.
4. Preheat the Air Fryer to 370-390 F
5. Place meatballs into the air fryer and cook for 8-10 minutes, depending on the size of your meatballs.

# Pork Loin with Potatoes and Herbs

**Prep time**: 10 minutes

**Cook time**: 25-30 minutes

**Servings**: 2

**Ingredients**

- 2-pound pork loin
- 2 large potatoes, large dice
- ½ teaspoon garlic powder
- ½ teaspoon red pepper flakes
- 1 teaspoon dried parsley, crushed
- ½ teaspoon black pepper, freshly ground
- A pinch of salt
- Balsamic glaze to taste

**Directions**

1. Sprinkle the pork loin with garlic powder, red pepper flakes, parsley, salt, and pepper.

2. Preheat the air fryer to 370 F and place the pork loin, then the potatoes next to the pork in the basket of the air fryer and close. Cook for about 20-25 minutes.
3. Remove the pork loin from the air fryer. Let it rest for a few minutes before slicing.
4. Place the roasted potatoes to the serving plate. Slice the pork. Place 4-5 slices over the potatoes and drizzle the balsamic glaze over the pork.

# Country Fried Steak

**Prep time**: 10 minutes

**Cook time**: 12-15 minutes

**Servings: 2**

**Ingredients**

- 2 pieces 6-ounce sirloin steak pounded thin
- 4 eggs, beaten
- 1 - ½ cup all-purpose flour
- 1 - ½ cup breadcrumbs
- 1 teaspoon onion powder
- 1 teaspoon garlic powder
- 1 teaspoon salt
- ½ teaspoon pepper

**Directions**

1. Combine the breadcrumbs, onion, and garlic powder, salt and pepper.
2. In other bowls place flour and beat eggs.

3. Dip the steak in this order: flour, eggs, and seasoned breadcrumbs.
4. Cook breaded steak for 6-7 minute at 380 F, turn over once and cook for another 5-7 minutes until becomes golden and crispy.

# Beef with Broccoli

**Prep time**: 5 minutes

**Cook time**: 25 minutes

**Servings**: 4

**Ingredients**

- 2 pounds beef
- 4 cups broccoli florets
- 1 large onion, cut into wedges
- 2 - 1/2 tablespoons cornstarch, divided
- 1/2 cup water
- 2 garlic cloves, minced
- 1 tablespoons vegetable oil
- 1/3 cup reduced sodium soy sauce
- 2 tablespoons brown sugar
- 1 teaspoon ground ginger
- 1/2 teaspoon salt

**Directions**

1. Mix in a large bowl cornstarch, water, minced garlic.
2. Cut beef into 6mm wide strips and soak in the mixture.
3. Put beef into the air fryer, sprinkle with oil and cook for 10 minutes in 350 F. Remove and set aside.
4. Add broccoli and onion to the air fryer sprinkle with oil and cook for 8 minutes.
5. Combine in a bowl ginger, brown sugar, soy sauce, remaining cornstarch and water.
6. Add beef and sauce mixture to the air fryer and cook for 6-8 minutes.

# Quick & Easy Meatballs

**Prep time**: 10 minutes

**Cook time**: 20 minutes

**Servings**: 4

**Ingredients**

- 1 - 1/2 pound minced meat (mixture of 80% veal and 20% pork)
- 1 teaspoon ground cumin
- 3 oz gruyere cheese
- 2 slices white bread
- 3 1/2 fl oz milk
- 4-5 sprigs parsley
- 1 egg
- 1 - 3/4 oz flour
- Salt to taste

**Directions**

1. Add minced meat and one bitten egg in the bowl.

2. Soak bread in a warm milk and add it to the meat.
3. Add to the mixture cumin and chopped parsley. Mix vigorously with a fork, season to taste.
4. Roll small meatballs with hands. Stuff each meatball with a small piece of cheese and close meatball up to avoid running cheese out while cooking.
5. Roll meatballs in a flour and cook them in several batches in the air fryer in 340 F for 20 minutes.

# Char Siu

**Prep time**: 5 minutes

**Cook time**: 15 minutes

**Servings**: 3

**Ingredients**

- 1 pound pork
- 3 tablespoon hoisin sauce
- 3 tablespoon sugar
- 3 tablespoon soy sauce
- 2 tablespoon corn syrup
- 2 tablespoon mirin
- 2 tablespoon olive oil
- Salt and pepper to taste

**Directions**

1. Cut pork into 2-inch stripes.

2. Mix all ingredients besides oil together in a large bowl and then put the meat into marinade. Set aside at least for 40 minutes.
3. Discard marinade and sprinkle pork with olive oil.
4. Cook in the air fryer preheated to 380 F for 15 minutes.
5. Serve.

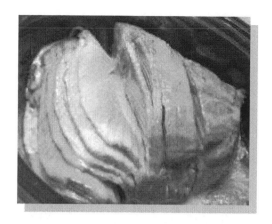

# Drunken Ham with Mustard

**Prep time**: 10 minutes

**Cook time**: 40 minutes

**Servings**: 4

### Ingredients

- 1 joint of ham, approximately 1 - 1/2 pound
- 2 tablespoon honey
- 2 tablespoon French mustard
- 8 oz whiskey
- 1 teaspoon Provencal herbs
- 1 tablespoon salt

### Directions

1. In a large casserole dish that fits in your Air Fryer prepare the marinade: combine the whiskey, honey and mustard.
2. Place the ham in the oven dish and turn it in the marinade.

91

3. Preheat the Air Fryer to 380 F and cook the ham for 15 minutes.
4. Add another shot of whiskey and turn in the marinade again. Cook the ham for 25 minutes until done.
5. Serve with potatoes and fresh vegetables.

# Delicate Steak with Garlic

**Prep time**: 10 minutes

**Cook time**: 30 minutes

**Servings**: 3

## Ingredients

- 1 pound halibut steak
- 2/3 cup soy sauce
- ¼ cup sugar
- ½ cup Japanese cooking wine
- 2 tablespoons lime juice
- 1 garlic clove, crushed
- ¼ cup orange juice
- ¼ teaspoon ground ginger
- ¼ teaspoon crushed red pepper flakes
- ½ teaspoon salt

## Directions

1. All ingredients mix in a saucepan and make a fine marinade
2. Bring to a boil over high heat. Divide in halves.
3. One half of the marinade put with the halibut in releasable bag and set aside in the refrigerator for 30 minutes.
4. Preheat the air fryer to 390°F and cook marinated steak for 10-12 minutes.
5. The other half of the marinade serves with cooked steak.

# Fish & Seafood Recipes

## Deep Fried Coconut Shrimps

**Prep time**: 10 minutes

**Cook time**: 20 minutes

**Servings**: 3-4

**Ingredients**

- 15-20 large shrimps, deveined and peeled
- 16 oz coconut milk
- 1 cup breadcrumbs
- 1 cup coconut, shredded
- Ground pepper and salt for seasoning

**Directions**

1. Add a pinch of salt in a coconut milk, whisk and set aside.

2. Combine breadcrumbs with shredded coconut, add salt and pepper to taste.
3. Preheat the Air Fryer to 330 F
4. Dip each shrimp in the milk mixture, then coat with coconut mix.
5. Place shrimps in the fryer and cook for nearly 20 minutes.

# Crispy Air Fryer Fish

**Prep time**: 10 minutes

**Cook time**: 12-15 minutes

**Servings**: 4

**Ingredients**

- 4 fish fillets (as you desired)
- 1 egg, whisked
- 3 oz breadcrumbs
- 2 tablespoon olive oil
- 1 lemon to serve

**Directions**

1. Whisk one egg and set aside.
2. Mix olive oil and breadcrumbs. Stir to combine until becomes loose and crumbly.
3. Preheat the Air Fryer to 360 F

4. Dip fish fillets into whisked egg and then into the breadcrumbs mixture. Make sure that fillets fully breaded.
5. Cook fillets for 12-15 minutes. Cooking time may vary depending on the fillets thickness.

# Asian Salmon with Fried Rice

**Prep time**: 5 minutes

**Cook time**: 10 minutes

**Servings**: 3-4

**Ingredients**

- 1 pound salmon fillet
- 2 cup cooked rice
- 3 large eggs, beaten
- 2 tablespoon olive oil
- 3 garlic cloves, minced
- 2 tablespoon frozen mixed vegetables
- 2 sprig spring onions, chopped
- 1 - ½ teaspoons sambal chili
- 1 tablespoon light soy sauce
- 3 teaspoon seasoning for salmon (as you prefer)
- A pinch of salt

## Directions

1. Season fish fillets on both sides and set aside. Cook salmon fillet skin side up at 360 F for couple minutes till 80% done. Replace to a large plate.
2. Add some oil to the air fryer basket and fry garlic till fragrant, 1-2 minutes. Add the frozen mixed vegetables and cook for a minute more. Add salmon pieces.
3. Then add all the rice and stir fry quickly to combine. Pour in the soy sauce and sambal chili. Mix well. Make some space in the middle of the rice and crack the eggs. Allow to set for 30 seconds then combine with all the rice. Keep tossing to keep things going. Add the chopped spring onions.
4. Continue frying on high heat until salmon ready and rice golden.

# Cod Fish Teriyaki with Oyster Mushrooms

**Prep time**: 5 minutes

**Cook time**: 12 minutes

**Servings**: 2-3

## Ingredients

- 1 pound cod fish cut into 1-inch thickness pieces
- 6 pieces Oyster mushrooms, sliced
- 1 Wong Bok leaf, sliced
- 2 garlic cloves, coarsely chopped
- 1 tablespoon olive oil
- A pinch of salt
- Steamed rice for serving

## DIY Teriyaki sauce

- 2 tablespoon mirin
- 2 tablespoon soy sauce
- 2 tablespoon sugar

## Directions

101

1. Take a large baking pan suitable for your air fryer and grease it with the little oil.
2. Toss your mushroom, garlic and salt with 1 tablespoon of oil in a baking pan. Lay the cod fish slices on top of mushrooms.
3. Preheat the Air Fryer at 360 F and place the baking pan into the air fryer. Cook for 5 minutes. Then, stir the mushrooms to prevent sticking and burning. Some mushroom parts may have browned slightly and it is ok.
4. Drizzle Teriyaki sauce over cod fish slices. Fry for another 5 minutes.
5. When ready, transfer cod fish slices to serving plate.
6. Stir the mushrooms with the remaining sauce in the baking pan.
7. Serve with steamed rice.

# Shrimps Fried with Celery

**Prep time**: 5 minutes

**Cook time**: 13 minutes

**Servings**: 2-3

**Ingredients**

- 6-8 stalks celery
- 1 small carrot
- 10-12 fresh shrimps
- 3 clove garlic, finely chopped
- 1 tablespoon olive oil
- 1 tablespoon oyster sauce
- 1 tablespoon soy sauce
- 1 teaspoon sugar
- 1 teaspoon cornstarch
- 3/4 to 1 cup water

**Directions**

1. Preheat the air fryer to 350 F.

103

2. Put chopped garlic, sliced diagonally celery and sliced carrot into the air fryer, pour with oil and cook for 7 minutes.
3. Mix oyster sauce, soy sauce, sugar, cornstarch and water in a bowl. Add this mixture into the air fryer and cook for another 1-2 minutes.
4. Add shrimps and cook for another 5 minutes.

# Crispy Nachos Shrimps

**Prep time**: 20 minutes

**Cook time**: 10 minutes

**Servings**: 2-3

**Ingredients**

- 20 shrimps
- 2 eggs
- 7 oz nacho flavored chips

**Directions**

1. Remove the shells and veins from the shrimps
2. Place eggs in the bowl and whisk.
3. Crush nacho chips in another bowl.
4. Dip each shrimp in the whisked egg and then in the chips crumbs.
5. Cook crumbled shrimps in the air fryer at 370 F for 8 minutes.

# Cod Fish Bites

**Prep time**: 10 minutes

**Cook time**: 8 minutes

**Servings**:

**Ingredients**

- 2 cod fish fillets
- ½ cup all-purpose flour
- 3 eggs
- 2 garlic cloves, minced
- 2 small chili peppers, chopped
- 2 spring onions, chopped
- ¼ teaspoon black pepper
- A pinch of salt

**Directions**

1. Whisk 3 eggs and add chopped green onion, garlic, and chili. Season with salt and black pepper.
2. Cut the fillets into 2 inch pieces.
3. Coat cod pieces with flour and then dip into the egg mixture.
4. Cook cod pieces into the air fryer for 7-8 minutes at 390 F

# Sugar Glazed Salmon

**Prep time**: 7 minutes

**Cook time**: 15 minutes

**Servings**: 3

**Ingredients**

- 3 salmon filets
- 1 tablespoon brown sugar
- 2 tablespoons coconut oil, melted
- Salt and pepper to taste

**Directions**

1. Combine in a middle bowl melted coconut oil with brown sugar, mix and season with salt and pepper.
2. Preheat the Air Fryer to 350 F
3. Dip salmon filets to the mixture. Be careful and try not to destroy tender salmon.
4. Put the glazed salmon into the air fryer and cook approximately 15 minutes.

108

# Salmon with Soy Sauce

**Prep time** 5 minutes

**Cook time**: 10 minutes

**Servings**: 2

**Ingredients**

- 1 pound salmon steaks
- ¼ cup brown sugar
- 4 tablespoon soy sauce
- 2 tablespoons olive oil
- 2 tablespoons fresh lemon juice
- 3 tablespoons dry white wine
- Lemon wedges for serving
- Salt to taste

**Directions**

1. Combine soy sauce, olive oil, brown sugar, wine, and lemon juice. Stir until the sugar dissolves.

109

2. Dip salmon steaks into the mixture, leave for 10 minutes.
3. Preheat the Air Fryer to 380 F
4. Then place salmon into a heatproof dish, season with salt to taste, put into the air fryer cooking basket and cook for 10 minutes.
5. Serve with lemon wedges and enjoy.

# Dessert Recipes

## Blueberry Muffins

**Prep time**: 25 minutes

**Cook time**: 15 minutes

**Servings**: 2-3

### Ingredients

- 3 oz flour
- 1 egg
- 3 oz milk
- 2 oz butter, melted
- 4 oz dried blueberries
- 1 teaspoon cinnamon
- 3 tablespoons brown sugar

### Directions

1. In the large bowl sift the flour, add cinnamon, sugar and stir to combine.

111

2. In another bowl whisk one egg with milk and add melted butter. Mix well and stir this mixture in the flour.
3. Add dried blueberries to the mixture.
4. Put the batter into the muffin cups.
5. Preheat the Air Fryer to 380 F
6. Carefully place filled muffin cups to the air fryer basket and set the timer to 15 minutes.
7. Bake muffins until they become golden brown.
8. Cool and serve.

# Chocolate Chips Cookies

**Prep time**: 5 minutes

**Cook time**: 8-9 minutes

**Servings**: 5-6

## Ingredients

- 5 tablespoon unsalted butter
- 4 tablespoon brown sugar
- 1 cup self raising flour or less
- 4 oz chocolate
- 1-2 tablespoon honey
- 1 tablespoon skimmed milk
- A pinch of vanilla extract

## Directions

1. Combine softened butter, sugar and mix together until they are light and fluffy. Stir in honey, flour and vanilla extract and mix well.

2. Using a rolling pin smash up your chocolate so that they are a mix of medium and really small chocolate chunks. Add the chocolate to the mixture. Also pour in the milk and stir well.
3. Preheat the Air Fryer to 370 F. Spoon the cookies into the air fryer on a baking sheet and cook for 5-6 minutes. Reduce the temperature to 330 F and cook additionally for 2 minutes so that they can cook in the middle.

# Amazing Coconut Cookies

**Prep time**: 7 minutes

**Cooking time**: 12 minutes

**Servings**: 2-3

## Ingredients

- 1 egg
- 3 tablespoons dried coconut
- 3 oz butter
- 2 oz brown sugar
- 1 teaspoon vanilla extract
- 2 oz white chocolate
- 5 oz flour

## Directions

1. Mix butter and brown sugar. Cream until fluffy.
2. Add one egg, vanilla extract and stir to combine.
3. Crush the chocolate into small pieces. Add them to the mixture.

115

4. Roll small balls with hands.
5. Roll these balls in the dried coconut cover.
6. Place balls on the baking sheet.
7. Preheat the Air Fryer to 370 F
8. Bake coconut balls for 8 minutes.
9. Lower the temperature to 280-300 F and cook for another 4 minutes.

# Fried Apple Dumplings

**Prep time**: 10-12 minutes

**Cook time**: 25 minutes

**Servings**: 2-3

## Ingredients

- 2-3 medium apples
- 2 tablespoon raisins
- 1 – ½ tablespoon brown sugar
- 2 sheets puff pastry
- 3 tablespoon butter, melted
- 1 teaspoon icing sugar for topping

## Directions

1. Core and peel apples.
2. Mix the raisins and the brown sugar.
3. Put each apple on one of the puff pastry sheet then fill the core with the raisin and sugar mixture. Fold the pastry around the apple so it is fully covered.

117

4. Place the apple dumplings on a small sheet of foil (to avoid any juices escape from the apple and don't fall into the air fryer). Brush the dough with the melted butter.
5. Cook apples for about 20-25 minutes at 370 F, until becomes golden brown and the apples are soft.
6. Top with icing sugar and serve hot.

# Apple Chips

**Prep time**: 10 minutes

**Cook time**: 20 minutes

**Servings**: 4

**Ingredients**

- 4 large apples
- 1 cup rolled oats (quick cook if possible)
- 1 teaspoon butter, melted
- 1 teaspoon cinnamon
- 2 teaspoon brown sugar
- 1 teaspoon olive oil

**Directions**

1. Wash and dry apples, peel them and remove cores.
2. Mix melted butter, brown sugar and oats.
   Cut apples into slices, put into the air fryer, sprinkle mixture around the apples and cook for 10-15 minutes at 340 F.

# Conclusion

Thank you for purchasing my air fryer cookbook! Hope all of the recipes from this guide were helpful and you got real pleasure and satisfaction cooking them.

**Note from the author:**

*If you've enjoyed this book, I'd greatly appreciate if you could leave an honest review on Amazon.*

*Reviews are very important to us authors, and it only takes a minute for to post.*